The Pyjama Par
A Play

June Crebbin

Illustrated by Peter Kavanagh

Characters

 Emma

 Dad *Emma's father*

 Mum *Emma's mother*

 Jess *Emma's friend*

 Alice *Jess's sister*

 Tom *Emma's brother*

 **CAMBRIDGE**
UNIVERSITY PRESS

Scene 1

At tea-time

Emma   In two weeks it's my birthday!

Mum   What kind of party do you want, Emma?

Dad   How about a pyjama party?

Emma   Yes! We can all wear pyjamas!

Dad   You can have a pillow fight.

Emma   Yes! Good idea!

Scene 2

Two weeks later, in the morning

Dad   Happy birthday, Emma! Is that a new jumper?

Emma   Yes – it's from Grandma. I love the horse!

Tom   What are these?

Mum   Jam tarts for tea.

Tom   Yummy! Can I have one?

Mum   No! They're for the party.

Scene 3

In the afternoon

Emma   Let's put our pyjamas on!

Tom   I don't want to wear pyjamas.

Emma   Everyone is going to wear pyjamas. It's a *pyjama* party.

Later

Jess   Happy birthday, Emma.

Emma   Oh, a pencil case. It's lovely. Thank you!

Alice   Happy birthday, Emma.

Emma   Oh, a picture of a horse. It's lovely. Thank you!

Emma   Let's dance!

Dad turns on the music. Everyone dances.

Jess   This is fun! I love dancing.

Alice   So do I!

Emma   It's a disco!

Emma   Now let's have a pillow fight.

Dad   Put your teddy on your head. I say "GO!" and you hit your friend with your pillow. When your friend's teddy falls off, you win!

Emma and Jess fight.

Dad   Be careful, Emma!

Emma hits a jug of flowers.

Emma   Oh, no! I'm sorry.

Mum   What a mess!

Dad   Time for tea, I think.

Scene 4

After tea

Jess   Ooh, I'm full!

Tom   Can I have another jam tart, Mum?

Mum   Not another one, Tom! You can have one
              tomorrow.

Dad Time for the ghost story.

Everyone Oooooooooh!

Everyone sits on the carpet.

Alice I don't like ghost stories.

Dad Once upon a time, there was a house with a ghost. Every night the ghost flew round the house and looked through the windows.

Everyone Oooooooh!

A white face flies past the window.

Jess   Look! A white face!

Everyone Where?

Jess   At the window!

Dad   Every night, the ghost knocked on the windows.

              There is a knock at the window.

Emma   It's the ghost!

Alice   I don't like it.

              Jess and Emma run to the window.

              Mum pulls a white sheet off her head.

Mum   It's only me!

Emma   It's only Mum!

              Everyone laughs.

Emma   What did the ghost do, Dad?

Dad   It flew round and round the house, and then it flew to the moon, and no-one saw it again.

Everyone laughs.

Scene 5

At bedtime

Jess   I'm hungry.

Alice   Me too.

Emma   Let's get the jam tarts!

Jess and   Good idea.
Alice

The girls get out of bed.

Emma   Shh! Quiet!

Alice   I'm scared.

Jess   Look! There's something in Tom's room.

They open Tom's door.

Jess   It's Tom! He's having a disco!

Alice   And he's eating.

Emma   *Our* jam tarts!

Tom   I'm having *my* pyjama party. Do you want a jam tart?

Everyone laughs.